CITY
GARDEN

F

FRANCES LINCOLN LIMITED
PUBLISHERS

CITY
GARDEN

ANDI CLEVELY

PHOTOGRAPHY BY
STEVEN WOOSTER

Frances Lincoln Ltd
4 Torriano Mews
Torriano Avenue
London NW5 2RZ
www.franceslincoln.com

City Garden
Copyright © Frances Lincoln 2008
Text copyright © Andi Clevely 2008
Photographs copyright
© Steven Wooster 2008

First Frances Lincoln edition: 2008

A catalogue record for this book is
available from the British Library.

ISBN 978-0-7112-2785-9

Printed and bound in Singapore

9 8 7 6 5 4 3 2 1

City gardens offer privacy in various
ways: for example, a virtual assertion
of personal space (page 1); the solid
seclusion of a creeper-clad walled
garden (page 2); or an serene sunlit
panorama of fresh greenery just a
step or two away (right).

CONTENTS

INTRODUCTION

Urban gardens are very special places. Individually they matter because each is a personal outdoor space, often a cherished refuge within densely built-up surroundings, somewhere all your own to be used, enjoyed and embellished according to need or fancy. Collectively they make up a vital and extensive green mosaic in an otherwise hard and uncompromising landscape, where nature can sometimes seem far away.

Often demeaned in estate agents' literature by the bland and aloof phrase 'garden attached', city plots may be almost any shape, size or form imaginable, from the lawns and dappled tree shade of many suburban sites and some older town residences, to the token beds, minimal balconies and windy rooftop patios of inner-city developments. Despite their diversity, they all share the distinctive conditions imposed by an urban setting.

Vanishing spaces

Treasured since earliest civilizations as private havens and oases, sources of solace or inspiration, these countless pockets of foliage and fresh air now constitute an influential component of current efforts to 'green' cities and make living there a healthier and more enjoyable experience. Yet city gardens are also a threatened resource. Fewer new properties are built with private gardens because planners are under considerable pressure to increase housing densities and often create communal gardens and play areas instead. Although welcome as green spaces and certainly better than nothing, these offer little to residents who want a private outdoor retreat or the chance to participate in active gardening.

Existing back gardens are steadily disappearing as house extensions, new building and hard surfaces cover ever greater areas of open ground. Front gardens are increasingly transformed into spaces for cars in many towns and cities as roadside parking becomes more of an expensive lottery.

In the UK gardens are now redesignated as 'brownfield sites', which increases their vulnerability to development and makes it harder for town planners to refuse building applications. The relentless erosion of open space means that often less than one-third of the land area in many cities supports vegetation compared with over three-quarters in the suburbs.

Urban surroundings create a genial microclimate where tropical plants like cannas and castor oil (*Ricinus*) often flourish almost all year (page 6) and a host of mixed shrubs, climbers, aquatics and herbaceous plants spread into a lush secret oasis (right).

Ironically, however, city gardens contain a much greater diversity of wildlife than most of the green fields planning laws are designed to protect. A surprisingly large and varied population of birds, mammals and other creatures have made themselves at home within cities, but their security is often tenuous and they deserve all the hospitality urban plots can offer. For many birds gardens are becoming a vital resource rather than an optional extra.

Benefits and challenges

With so much green space disappearing it becomes more crucial to preserve and tend the remaining areas, and even to extend them by making greater use of roofs, walls and the sides of buildings to grow plants and introduce a little more of the natural world into densely settled areas, benefiting residents and wildlife alike.

Keen gardeners are likely to cherish the space available to them, regardless of its size and situation, and have usually learned to turn perceived difficulties of gardening in the city to advantage. The well-known 'heat island' effect in urban areas ensures milder temperatures, and there is often higher rainfall over a greater number of days, and with every plant consequently making a joyful,

The essential elements of larger gardens – plants, paving, water, even turf – co-exist amiably in this small walled city plot, softening the built surroundings and introducing both peace and profusion.

almost defiant gesture of vitality, even modest gardening efforts can make an impact on barren surroundings. Non-gardeners, too, welcome a personal space outdoors as a tranquil refuge and antidote to work stress or hot, noisy and tiring streets.

So venture beyond any first impressions of apparent handicaps such as lack of space or privacy, traffic noise or unsympathetic surroundings – as this book explains, there are many ways to accommodate or counter these influences – and instead discover the assets, advantages and extra planting opportunities of the milder, more sheltered urban world.

Far from being a constraint, restricted space often leads to a more intimate and satisfying focus on fewer but more-prized specimen plants, which can include unusual, exotic or extravagant species likely to sulk or succumb in less favoured surroundings. Vertical surfaces and roofs can become potential growing areas, greening the surroundings, improving the local microclimate and countering the insidious effects of traffic pollution. And even in a small space you can nurture a whole profusion of food crops on your own back doorstep, often all year round. On balance a garden in a city environment can be as fulfilling and absorbing as in any other location, and offers a range of opportunities for open-air living, working or playing, whether as a small green patch of charming disorder, a calming sanctuary or a private stage for entertainment, dining and family activities alfresco.

The enclosed garden

A medieval monastic garden was typically small, severely square or rectangular, and bounded on all sides by the high walls of monastery buildings, which conferred a sense of peace and security on the green enclosure or *hortus conclusus*. Raised beds edged with boards and terraces round the sides contained an essential collection of favourite plants. The walls would bear trained fruit trees, aromatic herbs perfumed the air and enticed bees and butterflies, a corner seat encouraged quiet contemplation, and the beds were sometimes divided by little canals of still water to sustain fish and help irrigate the plants. It might be the perfect model for a modern city garden.

1

EXPLORING the CITY GARDEN

Undervalued by some and disparaged by others unaware of their distinctive qualities, city gardens are in fact priceless spaces that help breathe fresh life into urban surroundings. Explore the unique character of your particular patch, whether it is a high-rise window box, enclosed courtyard or token front garden in a busy street, and start to discover its ability to become a source of relaxation, seasonal change and natural beauty in an artificial environment.

GETTING YOUR BEARINGS

Take a long, detached look round your garden and consider its qualities and failings systematically. You might be able to appraise it at a glance or, if it is large or established, need more time to investigate remote or hidden corners. If you have lived there for some time, of course, you'll be familiar already with some of its delights and drawbacks, but it is always worth considering

options for improvement, sometimes by exploring beyond conventional ideas and assumptions. A garden you have just taken over will need more careful assessment from all angles – literally: stand at the end and study its appearance as you face the house, for example; look upwards, because influences and opportunities come from overhead as well as from adjacent properties; and also assess the view from any upstairs windows.

Evaluate what you have got, and start to jot down thoughts about what you'd like.

Note the most striking features, such as a slope or view, high walls or trees, or perhaps just a sense of abandoned space ripe for clearance and improvement. Do you need all the existing features? Could you perhaps adapt, restore or move them, or would it be simpler to clear the

As cities are essentially workplaces, it is not surprising that city gardens often emphasize rest and renewal. At rooftop level (above and page 12) planted gathering places lift leisure-time relaxation above the daily routine.

Natural landscape materials like worn pebbles and moving water, with the addition of a few choice container plants, will transform even a sterile and unpromising leftover place between buildings into an inviting courtyard cloister. Discreet artificial lighting prolongs enjoyment beyond dusk.

site completely and start afresh? Remember that where space is confined clutter is often oppressive, and that less can actually be more, offering space, air and room to manoeuvre.

Test the atmosphere of the garden. An established plot might benefit from more light or shade; it could seem dark and unfriendly, or possibly small and sterile if simply turfed or concreted all over. This is your territory on which to stamp your personality: everything in it needs to work hard (unless space is no object) and its appraisal deserves as much thought as any other room in the house.

Assess influences from without. Neighbours to the side or on higher floors might overlook you; adjacent buildings or hedges could overshadow all or part of the garden. A roof garden or balcony will often feel uncomfortably exposed to the elements, even if the view is glorious. If your garden is a basement area, is it all darkness and moss, can you see much of the sky and is it important to preserve or enhance this outlook? Front gardens serve many purposes, from giving the house a setting or shielding it from public view to providing security or a convenient off-road parking area. Would you feel uncomfortable gardening in yours regularly or maybe prefer just a passive, easily tended boundary between house and street?

Open-air pleasures are many and various: here a secluded corner has been developed as a decked patio for a hot tub, enclosed by a timber pergola and trellis screen, plus a variety of evergreens and seasonal bedding plants.

Weigh up practical aspects, such as easy access from the street and to all parts of the garden. Will you need to take a wheelbarrow down to the allotment, perhaps, or negotiate a pushchair to and from the back door. Will you have to cater for other family members and their different interests and activities? Are you happy to commit yourself to the regular tasks of practical gardening, or is low maintenance a high priority?

Feeling your way

Devote plenty of time to looking around and becoming familiar with your garden, and let your thoughts and reactions mellow: a change of weather or mood could alter first impressions dramatically. Allow an outline of a plan to evolve gradually; don't be too dogmatic or detailed at this stage. Chapter 2 suggests some of the many possible strategies for adapting and reinventing what you've got, and it's important to stay receptive to ideas before initiating major changes. If inspiration falters, you can always consult a professional designer who specializes in city gardens.

SPECIAL SITES

Although a garden is widely assumed to be a piece of accessible and cultivable open ground, in town it might be little more than a concreted courtyard, a flat roof high above neighbouring buildings or perhaps a collection of pots, hanging baskets and window boxes on a small balcony, far from any natural amenities. But despite their apparent limitations, each offers promises and possibilities.

Courtyard Sometimes no more than a left-over space between buildings, a courtyard can be an important light well within shaded surroundings and a protected heat trap for much of the year. Depending on the style and condition of its floor surface, you may need to add little more than some planting for colour, lighting and appropriate furniture to transform it into the perfect setting for dining, relaxing or partying alfresco. Stage a few significant plants in bold containers or build more extensive raised beds to satisfy practical gardening aspirations. Reserve patches of soil for possible planting. If a floor surface is disintegrating, you might need to hire a breaker to reduce it to rubble and start afresh.

Roof garden An exciting garden in the sky, a roof garden often has spectacular views but also harsher living conditions unless moderated by an enclosure of parapet walls; any extreme exposure will mean that you need to provide some kind of screening against sun and wind.

Hard-surfaced passageways, courtyards and urban atria offer special opportunities for creativity with daring colour, bold positioning of *objets d'art* or specimen plants, and the imaginative use of flooring materials like bricks, aggregates, tiles and mosaic tesserae.

Plants need selecting for drought tolerance and usually have to be grown in containers which, like seating and other furnishings, should be lightweight and stable – *always* check structural stability before adding any substantial extra weight. A well-planted roof garden can provide you with privacy and shelter, visual appeal and environmental benefits far beyond your boundary.

Balcony A common feature of multiple dwellings, a balcony shares many of the qualities of a roof garden, although aspect is more influential, depending on which direction it faces. Plants have to be grown in containers standing on the balcony floor or attached to walls and railings. There may be room to sit out in the open, and even for a small pond or wildflower collection. On the other hand lack of floor space may confine your activities to creating a miniature garden for viewing from indoors. A balcony garden will also become a neighbourhood amenity, redefining and enhancing the whole appearance of the building, especially if you train climbers and trailers on adjacent surfaces. The same precautions about structural strength apply to balconies as to roofs.

Basement A sunken area may seem a disheartening location to develop. It may have permanent shade and cold damp air, which often lodges stubbornly below circulating winds. Reclaim such a space with bright or warm colours, reflective materials and discreet artificial

A multi-level garden for all seasons and activities, lavishly appointed with spacious dining and rest areas, a small but inviting lawn for games and gatherings, a private corner summerhouse and a selection of undemanding but attractive plants to relieve the built environment.

Some key considerations

- In your available space, will you chiefly want to grow plants, entertain outdoors or simply sit at ease in the open air – or perhaps a combination of all these activities?
- Do you actually enjoy gardening, or might a few easy-care container plants and perhaps a water feature be sufficient natural ingredients?
- Does your neighbourhood offer alternative outdoor facilities: a park for recreation or allotments for growing food, perhaps?
- Is your property subject to any restraints – about planting trees, erecting fences or lighting barbecues, for example?
- Are there special issues you must take into account, such as young children and their play equipment, disability and the need for easy access, or having to allow space for parking?
- If your budget is tight, can you afford to pay for alterations? Or do you have the skill or inclination to do them yourself?

lighting. Plants need to be determined shade-lovers (of which there are many – see page 94), or possibly less shade tolerant if you can also stage containers on stairs or attached to walls, closer to some sunlight. Beware of trapped frost in a hard winter, but rejoice in your cool green retreat in high summer.

Community garden Some developments offer a communal area rather than private gardens. It can be difficult to relate to a shared expanse of mown grass and formally planted trees, and even individual patches may be subject to planting or fencing restrictions in the interests of uniformity. However, residents are sometimes able to combine and together actively cultivate a specially reserved area; gardening at the rear of a property is usually less stringently regulated. If all else fails, you may be able to deploy baskets, planters and window boxes close to home, and rent a neighbourhood allotment for more ambitious projects (not necessarily growing food crops).

MATTERS OF SCALE

Although minimal outdoor space is a reality for most people in the city, this need not cause dismay: there are

benefits to balance the obvious drawbacks. Very often the more unpromising a site looks, the greater the satisfaction to be derived from creating somewhere special and personal.

Size has very little to do with quality, as many gardeners have proved by transforming a mere scrap of ground into a celebration of small-scale gardening. Where space is cramped, choice becomes more discriminating: getting rid of clutter is liberating, and every plant or feature must earn its keep and will be treasured for its distinctive value. There may not be scope for endless pottering, but this

An old wall is an asset to cherish. Where its character and condition are impressive it is tempting to leave it exposed, but keep in mind that this can emphasize distance (opposite); camouflaging its extent with strategic plants here alters the scale of the same garden (above).

could suit a busy agenda or a preference for quick and easy maintenance.

When you first explore or reassess the garden space at your disposal, keep an open mind about its potential. There are many ways to expand (or reduce, if you wish, of course) the opportunities it offers. Be honest and unsentimental about your practical priorities (see panel page 22), consider how much time and stamina or enthusiasm you really have, and test these criteria against the reality of your particular patch to see how much you need to simplify or adapt, if at all.

Think divergently about your garden's potential. For example, plan in all three dimensions, upwards as well as horizontally, and consider varying ground levels to give at least the illusion of more space. Dividing the garden, however small, into separate areas has a similarly positive effect, as does laying paving or flooring in patterns or along an unexpected alignment (see page 44). Subdivision can make any garden more manageable and visually interesting.

Keep plans for the area bold and uncompromising. Small plants or beds in a small garden often look mean and diminished, whereas a few swaggering specimens can suggest profusion and expense; similarly a single generous bed will be more impressive as well as exaggerating the available space. Try tricking the eye with oversize architectural plants such as trachycarpus, cordylines, phormiums, astelia, agaves, fatsia or macleaya.

Wherever possible, allow for multipurpose use: stackable or fold-down furniture leaves potential room for play, box seats can supply storage space, dustbin or compost enclosures could support climbing plants or suspended pots. You might even be able to harmonize your overall design with dominant neighbouring features, such as a style of architecture, a tree, or even a chimney stack, so that the garden blends visually into the larger landscape while remaining essentially self-contained.

THE GARDEN MICROCLIMATE

Every garden has its own peculiar microclimate or set of environmental conditions, especially in town, where the built-up surroundings can confer shelter or cold draughts, cool shade or reflected sunlight, and hard ground surfaces absorb heat by day and then radiate it at night.

The overall effects of neighbourhood influences can be congenial for outdoor living generally and gardening in particular. Not only are urban areas noticeably milder than rural districts – they are referred to as 'heat islands' because of the dome of warm air that forms above them – but buildings and walls all act as storage heaters, radiating enough heat to raise temperatures as much as 6° C above the cooler countryside.

The same buildings, together with walls and trees, can slow or deflect winds, sheltering gardens from their worst effects, or alternatively funnel them between structures in violent gusts and locally turbulent eddies. More exposed gardens and balconies above ground may need permanent protection with plants or screens from the full force of rooftop winds.

Keen practical gardeners make small spaces work hard by exploiting vertical surfaces and even outbuildings as growing sites (below), adding containers of extra plants such as these succulents (right) when the ground area is full.

27

High plant-clad walls and a selection of medium-sized trees shield this semi-formal garden from wind, creating a protected microclimate where borderline-hardy agapanthus can flower carelessly and the combined scents of lavender and roses linger in the warm air.

Coping with strong winds

Erecting a solid baffle is often counter-productive, forcing gusts to swirl unpredictably over the top. The most practical windbreak is a partly permeable screen that filters and tames the wind rather than blocks it. Adding a 30cm (12in) high trellis strip along the top of existing walls and fences will reduce its impact. A hedge can be effective – where there is room and no risk of casting extra shade – and need not be tall, as it will shelter a distance up to ten times its height. A living fence or 'fedge' of stout wire mesh clad with evergreen climbers and trained shrubs occupies less space and can still reduce wind force by as much as three-quarters.

The warm air accumulating over cities contributes to a cloud cover 10 per cent greater than that in rural areas. Combined with a greater density of atmospheric particles, this can produce up to 30 per cent more rainfall on a higher number of wet days than there are in the country. This encourages plant growth and cools down surfaces, but also causes problems with sudden large surges of surface water during the higher incidence of heavy thunderstorms (see page 50).

This distinctive pattern of occasionally immoderate but generally benign weather conditions can make city gardening a stimulating proposition, offering opportunities for outdoor activity almost all year round in some places, as well as expanding the plant repertoire by permitting tender and borderline species to be grown successfully.

LETTING IN LIGHT

The amount of light in a city garden depends on its extent and the height of surrounding or included features and structures. Adequate light levels are essential for healthy plant growth as well as personal well-being, especially in winter when a garden at ground level may be permanently sunless and prolonged gloom can affect moods. Larger gardens, rooftops and balconies may be well lit all year round, depending on which direction they face.

The aspect of a garden or even an individual wall – the way it faces – affects its microclimate. In the northern

Congenial urban conditions favour a range of exciting exotic plants with which you can create a garden of lush foliage and rich colour. These include banana (*Musa basjoo*), bottlebrushes (*Callistemon*), castor oil plant (*Ricinus communis*), cordylines, crinodendron, fan palm (*Chamaerops humilis*), *Fatsia japonica*, ginger lilies (*Hedychium*), loquat (*Eriobotrya japonica*), tree fern (*Dicksonia antarctica*), climbers like clianthus, lapageria and *Cobaea scandens* (perennial in city gardens), and fruits such as carob, pistachio, olive, chayote, nectarines and kiwi fruit.

Protected by buildings and radiant heat from walls and paving, tender tree ferns, taro (*Alocasia*) and Italian cypresses (*Cupressus sempervirens*) enjoy a trouble-free existence.

hemisphere, south-facing gardens can be sunny and possibly very hot in high summer; a north-facing aspect will be gloomier but often pleasantly cool in summer; east-facing gardens receive the morning sun and some of the coldest winds; while a garden looking west could experience more rain and milder winds as well as presenting a view of the setting sun. Latitude, time of year and the amount of shade cast by trees and surrounding buildings will all modify these various light levels.

Shade can be a mixed blessing, offering a cool retreat from hot sun at one extreme, particularly in warmer regions, or Stygian gloom at the other. You can increase shade levels if you wish by erecting screens, growing climbers and planting trees (see page 98) – preferably deciduous species which admit extra light in winter while they are leafless.

How you can moderate shade depends on its source. Dominant boundary hedges and fences can be lowered (but don't compromise their value as security, noise baffles or windbreaks), while minor surgery can often transform darkness under trees into pleasantly dappled shade. Reduce excessive overshadowing from nearby buildings by deploying reflective materials wherever they can intercept light – examples include lime-washed walls, mirrors, still water features, plants with shiny surfaces and pale or reflective flooring and mulches such as crushed glass, ground metal or pulverized limestone.

Choose a comfortable sunny position for seating, but make sure this is portable: as the year progresses the angle and intensity of the sun changes, and in high summer your chosen spot could become an oven. Select appropriate plants that will enjoy and exploit each different aspect and the amount of light or shade available there.

Pruning for light

Neglected trees are a common source of unwanted shade. There are ways to alleviate this without harming the tree, but before starting any major work liaise with your neighbours if they are likely to be affected, and check that large mature trees are not covered by preservation orders (these allow reasonable maintenance or restoration work only). Don't take risks: employ a tree surgeon for cutting heavy boughs and any work much above head height.

Study the offending tree and then plan your strategy. To thin the canopy, cut out complete main branches one at a time, starting where the growth is densest, and assess results before continuing. Remove only up to one-third of the canopy in any single year. Shorten unduly long branches to leave a natural balanced shape all round. To lift the crown and admit more light from the sides, cut all lower branches from a bushy specimen, leaving a shapely top and clean stem or stems. Large overgrown shrubs like ceanothus, buddlejas and magnolias can be turned into small standard trees in the same way. Many deciduous trees and shrubs can be cut almost to ground level (coppiced) and will respond by producing numerous fresh, vigorous stems (in the case of shrubs) or more attractive foliage, which you can thin progressively to keep the topgrowth light and airy. Trees such as ash, oak, hazel and willow are traditionally managed in this

Where looming surroundings need disguise or concealment, aim for height and plenty: trees at eye level or above (left) attract attention and give an impression of size and profusion, while lavish climbers can turn an overlooked site (below) into a bosky refuge.

way every few years, while decorative shrubs that can be treated this way include dogwoods, catalpa, paulownia and ornamental elders.

THE WIDER CONTEXT

Almost inevitably gardening in a city means living in close proximity to other residents. People relate to their neighbourhood in a variety of ways. Some might welcome the sense of constant community and are happy to work outside, even in the front garden, and socialize with neighbours or passers-by. For many, though, the garden is a refuge, somewhere to unwind in private, away from the outside world with its insistent demands, noise and bustle.

Surrounding buildings, fences and hedges can confer isolation and prevent those outside from looking in, but you might equally well be overlooked by neighbours above or to the sides. If you crave seclusion, explore ways of screening off the outside world without contravening local regulations about the height of boundaries, annoying neighbours or creating shade problems or draughts.

Frosted plastic screens, trained plants and even bamboo blinds can enclose balconies and terraces, ensuring privacy as well as filtering or deflecting wind and noise. Overhead structures such as wires for climbers and trailers, a frosted glass veranda or even a giant garden parasol can screen a small private space within the garden. If you decide to plant a hedge, try native plants attractive to wildlife, such as cotoneaster, holly, gooseberries, berberis and buckthorn: prickly species help deter dogs and intruders, while those with berries attract birds.

In many towns boundary heights are tending to fall: the traditional 1.8m (6ft) fence can loom oppressively over a tiny garden and towering hedges are often regulated by by-laws. This trend can be beneficial, as lower boundaries may still shield or conceal a private sitting area while integrating the garden as a whole into the wider network of green spaces.

Interaction with neighbours can influence gardening habits, especially in a culturally diverse community, where international choices of flowers, vegetables and styles can quickly lead to a vibrant kind of fusion gardening. You may need to liaise over shared facilities such as a common fence or drive, an overhanging tree or invasive climber, and some familiar outdoor activities such as using a barbecue or garden machinery may constitute a social nuisance.

POLLUTION

All urban gardens are exposed in one way or another to pollution. The notorious industrial and domestic fuel smogs of post-war years have largely disappeared from many cities, only to be replaced by photochemical smogs from vehicle exhausts, visual pollution from street lighting and reflective building surfaces, and noise from a range of sources.

Plants for background sound

Countering intrusive noise with more pleasant sounds is often surprisingly effective, reducing the outside world to a background hum. Lively water features can often be 'tuned' to adjust the volume or produce more lyrical sounds, and the foliage of many plants will create a visual screen and whisper pleasingly as it moves in the breeze. Useful species for this purpose include bamboos such as non-rampant forms of *Fargesia*, *Pleioblastus* and *Sasa*, bladder senna (*Colutea arborescens*), cordylines, figs, flowering dogwood (*Cornus florida*), grasses such as *Cortaderia* and *Miscanthus*, lace-bark pine (*Pinus bungeana*), paper birch (*Betula papyrifera*), phormiums and Brewer's weeping spruce (*Picea breweriana*).

A model of cool simplicity, this garden is minimally furnished for quiet intimacy. A shield of clear glass bricks offers protection from noise and cool wind without hiding a borrowed landscape of luxuriant greenery.

Enclosed gardens are often shielded from the worst of these effects, although they can trap still, polluted air; front gardens lie open to most of these influences.

Plants are remarkably successful allies in any attempt to counter pollution, especially that of atmospheric gases and particles. Their leaves can filter as much as 85 per cent of these from the air, often passively intercepting them in leaf hairs from which rain washes them harmlessly into the soil.

Trees are the most efficient filters, notably deciduous kinds: their annual leaf fall bears pollutants safely to the ground and contributes to soil fertility. They also attenuate noise levels with their own soothing sounds, particularly at the frequencies to which the human ear is most sensitive.

Boundary hedges act as filters, while also screening out light and intruders. Covering surrounding walls with climbers has the same beneficial effects and can capture up to 6g per square metre (0.2oz per square yard) of pollutant dust. Once these trapped particles reach ground level, they are bound harmlessly in the soil or neutralized by bacteria, provided humus levels are kept high (see page 94).

Formality in three dimensions (below): soil-based hedging, topiary and exuberant climbers enclose a plain tiled patio laid diagonally to relieve any sense of predictability. When improved and enriched, city soils are equally capable of supporting a varied and vibrant community of informal cottage-garden plants (opposite).

GETTING TO KNOW YOUR SOIL

The wide variability of city garden soils is almost legendary. You could be lucky and take over from a dedicated gardener who has conscientiously nurtured the garden for years, but you might have a new site with builders' rubble covered by a veneer of bought-in topsoil, or inherit a wilderness of weeds, bare sterile earth or even a domestic rubbish dump. Fortunately with time and care all soils, no matter how abused or neglected, can be restored.

If you plan to grow plants, you should get acquainted with your soil type and its condition. First you might have to find it.

Plants against pollution

There may be as much as 12,000 dust particles per litre of air in a busy built-up townscape, compared with only 2,000 where there are plenty of plants. Resilient trees and shrubs to grow include acers, buddlejas, catalpa, ceanothus, cotoneaster, escallonia, hebes, holly, laburnum, lilacs, mulberries, osmanthus, periwinkles (*Vinca*), philadelphus, privet, prunus, robinia, symphoricarpos, tree of heaven (*Ailanthus altissima*), viburnum and weigela. Bearded irises, bergenias, coreopsis, crocosmia, dianthus, forget-me-nots, iberis, pelargoniums, petunias, tulips and most ferns are some tough herbaceous plants resistant to urban pollution.

If you need to clear rubble and waste or a legacy of established weeds, always proceed slowly: ours is an age of recycling, and other people's rejects may prove useful (see page 41), while weeds are prime compost material to be cleared with patience and turned into a valuable soil improver (see page 96). If the garden has been surfaced with gravel or some other loose material and you want to grow plants, rake enough to one side to expose the ground beneath.

To assess the soil, all you need initially is one or two small patches where you can dig a hole about 45cm (18in) deep and wide (you might have to do this anyway if you have brought bare-root plants with you that need temporary heeling in) to reveal the soil profile and check drainage.

The results of your preliminary test (see panel) may be unpredictable or simply confirm your initial suspicions. You could find stiff wet clay, thin dry soil or, more likely, something in between, but your discoveries will help you elaborate any plans and ambitions already in mind and suggest methods of ameliorating the soil's condition (see page 94).

If results seem depressing, remind yourself that no soil is totally lifeless, and most plants have evolved some ability to cope with challenging conditions. Note, too, that poor soil is often unfairly blamed for inadequacies that simply stem from bad weather, over-optimistic choice of plants or mistakes in their care.

Soil test

1. Dig a hole about 45cm (18in) deep and wide.
2. The side of your hole will reveal a 'profile' showing the depth of dark topsoil and the nature of the underlying subsoil, which is usually paler and possibly solid or plastic, if heavy clay, or gravelly if light and free-draining.
3. Test the drainage by pouring in two or three buckets of water. If it takes hours to seep away, you might need to provide a drainage system to avoid waterlogging in wet weather; or you could build raised beds instead.
4. While the topsoil is moist, squeeze a handful into a ball. Heavy clay keeps its moulded shape, feels sticky, may even by polished by your thumb; balls of light soil fall apart easily into loose grains with a gritty or sandy texture.

2

IMPROVING the CITY GARDEN

With urban populations being increasingly mobile the chances are that you have moved into a city residence with a garden that you want to tailor to your personal tastes and lifestyle. Even if you have managed the same garden for many seasons, there could be areas you want to remodel or enhance. Once you have weighed the merits and flaws of your city plot (see Chapter 1), you can review some of the many options for turning the garden into a private paradise of diversity and comfort.

PREPARING FOR CHANGE

Making the most of an urban garden means moving on from first impressions and exploring ways to redeem its failings and capitalize on its assets, and to modify its appearance in line with your aspirations.

Pause, though, before deciding on major upheaval: hasty decisions now could result in disappointment, problems or unnecessary expense later, and it would be prudent to consider the future as well as your immediate needs. Children and plants grow; energy and values change; your work might involve more entertaining at home or leave less free time to manage an exuberant plant collection. You

The garden is yours to alter and adapt according to your plans and preferences. Most of us want to organize the plot for multiple usage by plants and people (page 38 and above).

may want to deliberately include a certain amount of flexibility in your plans, leaving room for ideas to evolve.

- Start planning by reappraising your dreams realistically.
- Remember to involve everyone in your family, including their various needs or demands right from the start.

- Balance pleasure with practicality: a garden has to be made and maintained as well as admired.
- If you choose abundance rather than simplicity, make sure the garden will not end up tyrannizing you and will look as good as possible with minimum care.
- Equip it logically, making allowances for sitting out, drying washing, storing bicycles or play equipment, and all other family necessities.

Clearing rubbish

If the garden has been treated as a dump by previous owners, it will need cleaning up before you can do anything else. Sort the waste material methodically. Chemicals, plastic and toxic waste need safe disposal at a council tip. Scrap metal can be taken for recycling, although some items might be adapted for growing or supporting plants, or stacked and covered with scrambling plants as a wildlife habitat. Rocks, stones and broken concrete could make rock gardens, paths and edges, dry-stone walls or hardcore; car tyres make durable plant containers, improvised swings or simple steps when packed with soil or rubble. Pile rotting branches neatly as a haven for beetles and other small creatures, and compost all leaves, paper and plant debris.

- Decide whether you need to choose between plants and play, or if you have the space (and inclination) for both.
- Ask yourself if you (or a future resident) might later rue an irrevocable change, such as covering the ground with concrete or tarmac.

PLAYING WITH SPACE

Organizing the space at your disposal may seem a daunting, even frustrating challenge, especially if it is long and narrow, small and square, or, if it is a corner property, triangular or awkwardly irregular. Disguising limitations in size and shape depends on a combination of real and illusory measures.

Introducing different levels (see page 44) can increase real space, especially for growing plants, but make sure this does not restrict opportunities for outdoor entertaining or recreation, which usually require a level open area. Vertical surfaces can be used for plants, storage space and built-in seating. A raised bed could accommodate a pool, vegetables and trailing plants down the sides, together with seating along the edges. Sliding doors from the house save ground space that might be useful for containers, and allow house and garden to blend seamlessly without wasting the intervening ground. Whatever you decide, make the space work hard without thinking small.

A subtle play between horizontal blocks of walling and the vertical accents of clean tree trunks and solid sculpture disguises any limitations in this garden's size and shape.

Tricks of illusion deceive by apparently altering horizons and proportions, and by confusing boundaries, which always draw attention to themselves and immediately define the size of the garden. Concealing walls with plants and structures like latticework or panelling helps to disguise them, mirrors can suggest secret places beyond, and cunning use of colour can imply a sense of depth – painting a far wall with a dark shade, for example, fosters a sense of distance. To relieve an angular landscape and eliminate an awareness of corners and straight lines, introduce curves: a circular pool, bed or paved area is non-directional and focuses attention on its perimeter, emphasizing space rather than the garden setting.

Long and narrow

To divert the eye from instantly finding the end of long narrow plots, you can use various techniques. Subdividing the plot's length with screens of hedging, trellis, poles or woven hazel, willow or bamboo will create two or more 'rooms' that introduce an element of surprise and variety. Add a doorway or arched opening as an invitation to explore the unseen areas, each of which could be dedicated to a different activity – a dining area, wild garden, playground or a place for quiet withdrawal and early morning tai chi.

Simply extending borders out from the sides towards or even across the centre axis and planting them with tall shrubs can obscure the far end of the garden. Avoid a straight central path, which always accentuates length. Instead plan a meandering route or arrange paths at each side to exaggerate the sense of intervening space. Obscuring the end with plantings, a raised patio with a generous flight of steps or a creeper-clad arbour similarly shortens the perspective.

Small and square

Town gardens that are virtually enclosed courtyards, framed by highly architectural boundaries, need a strong design strategy to reduce their formal angularity. Plants are an important and versatile element in softening the walls and adding seasonal variety: tall shrubs, espalier fruit and climbers on lattice or trellis frames will break up blank surfaces and reduce feelings of oppression. You could drape complete walls with greenery (see page 104) to hide the boundary altogether and physically improve the atmosphere within the garden.

Paint bare walls with light colours to maximize solar gain, which will temper the chill of winter and evenings with absorbed sunlight, and to make the garden appear more cheerful and inviting. Adding mosaics, murals, wall ornaments or water features all helps to minimize hard-edged geometry.

When laying paving or decking, avoid echoing the square alignment of the walls by working on the diagonal: swinging the visual axis of pavers and joints to the longest dimensions (corner to corner) increases the illusion of space.

Alternatively try radiating strong directional lines in the floor to fan out from a doorway, perhaps using spines of tiles infilled with gravel and soil beds to defy the lie of the boundary.

Difficult shapes

Organizing a triangular or irregular-shaped garden needs a more experimental approach if you want to create a feeling of greater or more balanced space. Draw the outline of the garden on paper and then sketch in the features you want to retain or add, using contrasting shapes to break up the outline of the plot.

You might prefer a bold simple arrangement, setting a circular patio within a triangle, for example, and using the corners for flower beds or storage areas, a tree, shed or covered seat. Dividing the plot into smaller, more symmetrical areas might resolve the problem, or you could try doodling with a path that wanders gently from side to side, leading the eye from one feature to the next.

Visualize the design at ground level by daylight, from above if you have an upper floor, and at night if you plan lighting and evening entertainment, and play with shapes until you find a satisfying layout. Remember that in small

Illusion and artifice are acceptable techniques in every gardener's repertoire: here, deft positioning of the timber framework – itself a handsome and eye-catching structure – immediately hints at a special and separate space, like a room without walls.

spaces complexity and fussy detail rarely work as satisfactorily as understatement; construction and maintenance plans always need to be realistic; and the chosen design must look good all year round and meet your various needs, now and for the foreseeable future.

CHANGING LEVELS

Not all gardens are flat and level: many properties are built on the side of a hill or valley, and in mountainous areas the plot may be quite steep where it has been cut into a bank. Managing sloping or uneven ground requires caution, but such sites offer unique possibilities.

Urban gardens in hilly districts are usually at the back, with the land rising away from the house and therefore in full view – a distinct advantage over ground falling away from your line of vision. Gentle gradients offer few problems and may be planned as if on the level, although for comfort paths might have to climb the slope diagonally or rise in a series of shallow steps.

If the whole garden will be visible, it may be important to hide the far end from sight to imply distance. Alternatively abandon attempts to deceive and instead create a formal design that calls attention to the symmetrical ground plan, which will emphasize rather than camouflage the shape of the plot and also suggest a reassuring feeling of order and control on uneven terrain.

Steeper ground is liable to shed water and even soil in heavy rain and may become unstable if deeply disturbed, so get professional advice before attempting major earthworks. It may be possible to tend an existing bank as a natural garden by growing a variety of native plants, alpines or species shrubs, cutting a few simple steps for safe, comfortable access and aiming throughout for minimum maintenance.

Multi-level gardening

Even where the terrain is flat a change of level can introduce extra growing space or room for other activities. You can dig out an area at ground level to make a pool or sunken garden, for example, with seating at the edge and the excavated soil transferred to raised beds. Make sure, though, that you do not create drainage problems in the process or disturb underground utilities.

Terraces don't have to be straight or regular to organize sloping ground in practical, appealing ways. On a large scale they are most effective when following contours, while a more imaginative solution would be to build a totally contrasting shape, as here, where higher ground is transformed into a theatrical 'upper circle'.

Arranging a suite of terraced beds across or around a level garden provides complex levels for imaginative combinations of climbing, trailing and wall plants or for a cascading water world.

Terracing

A radical solution for a steep slope is to reshape it as a series of terraces running across the gradient, each level held back with a retaining wall or fence sturdy enough to prevent soil movement and equipped at its base with adequate drainage. Terraces can be planted as hanging gardens that allow climbers and ramblers to trail down in swags over the walls, as well as deploying arching and graceful shrubs or trees to enjoy from below.

Build wide safe steps up the slope, together with a handrail for safety. Arrange storage facilities close to the house to avoid unnecessary journeys uphill, but do consider providing seating at the top for you to enjoy any view, perhaps with enough room for dining and entertaining on high.

If local regulations and neighbourly relations permit, a tree house or multi-level structure can offer stimulating play space for children and dramatic planting opportunities above ground and even sturdy anchorage for a hammock. In heavily shaded basement areas building raised beds and planting shelves nearer the light and staging containers at the sides of steps will allow plants to be grown at several different levels and supplement meagre ground space.

BALCONY GARDENS

Its size may be modest, with no practical or even deceitful way to make it look bigger, but a balcony is in fact a privileged position, with unique appeal as somewhere almost literally out of this world.

Such above-ground sites usually avoid the shade problems of ground-level gardens, and even on the least sunny side of a building can receive enough light for plants to grow well. Plant care involves no digging or strenuous work, and there is often a stunning view as a ready-made backdrop.

Exposure is the main hazard, with wind a constant factor at height: this may need screening out with a

Balconies may vary in scale from extensive platforms to a narrow ledge behind a parapet, but they tend to have much in common – a tree-top view of the locality, for example, unobscured light, exposure to the elements and the need to grow plants in containers, whether capacious raised beds (left) or designer pots (below).

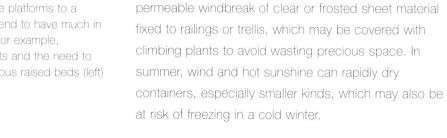

permeable windbreak of clear or frosted sheet material fixed to railings or trellis, which may be covered with climbing plants to avoid wasting precious space. In summer, wind and hot sunshine can rapidly dry containers, especially smaller kinds, which may also be at risk of freezing in a cold winter.

Nonetheless a balcony garden can give great pleasure, whether it is a tiny ledge with perhaps a miniature pool and a feeding station for urban birds or a large enough structure for you to equip as an outdoor room, with plenty of space for shrubs, trees, seating and other furniture. Make sure there are no structural dangers from heavy containers (reduce the weight of pots by adding a lightweight aggregate such as vermiculite to the compost) or floor surfacing such as pavers or floor tiles, and keep substantial weights close to load-bearing walls.

Plants are best grown in larger containers to lessen the frequency of watering – an important consideration where this needs carrying upstairs. Given shelter and careful attention to watering and feeding, most garden plants will thrive in high-rise positions, and you may be able to include a number of vegetables and herbs, and even small trees or shrubs to help ensure privacy and reinforce screening from wind.

HANGING GARDENS

For a curtain of foliage to soften a harsh city façade, plant up large pots with unrestrained climbers and allow these to clothe the balcony railings and trail downwards. Haul up the festoons annually and prune to an unobtrusive length. Hardy kinds, especially evergreens, will provide all-year-round charm and forage for birds, bees and butterflies, and can be supplemented with summer-flowering hanging basket annuals like sweet peas or trailing nasturtiums. Attractive climbers include Virginia creeper and Boston ivy (*Parthenocissus*), *Clematis vitalba*, aristolochia, jasmine, *Campsis radicans*, passionflowers, honeysuckles and ivies.

A solar windowsill

If your high-rise garden is just a window box, provided your window opens inward or has sliding sashes, you could improve its potential for growing flowers and small vegetables all year round – and also help warm the room inside – by constructing a miniature conservatory. Make a simple frame with a front, two ends and a sloping top, tailored to fit the top of the box and all round the window. Use 25mm (1in) square timber and clear plastic sheeting or rigid acrylic panels, and arrange a sliding or hinged panel for ventilation.

Water is a mercurial element that will instantly enliven barren urban surroundings, whether introduced as a congenial home for aquatic plants (far right) or as a playful landscape ingredient to supply music, movement and magical reflections by day or night (right).

WATER STRATEGIES

Every garden needs dry, all-weather surfaces for comfortable access, circulation and gathering places. While some gardeners are reluctant to spare ground for hard surfacing, and skimp on dimensions to save a little more growing space, in cities the trend is sometimes to the other extreme, with entire front gardens disappearing under paved parking areas and back gardens vanishing beneath patio floors and low-maintenance surfaces. As well as reducing the mosaic of green plots that is essential to urban well-being, an excess of paved areas can cause problems with rainwater dispersal.

Managing rainwater is a crucial factor in any garden scheme. Poorly drained ground can remain waterlogged for a long time, jeopardizing plant health and outdoor activity, and often leading to structural dampness; hard surfaces can shed up to three-quarters of rainfall rapidly, in volumes that overwhelm drainage systems and result in flash floods; and the changing climate promises more extreme and unpredictable weather events.

This garden is a happy blend of whimsical vision and skilful organization, its heart a still, almost contemplative landscape of water and rock forms in an undulating meadow of greenery (use plants like *Sagina* and *Raoulia* species), surrounded by lively borders packed with trees, shrubs and lush foliage of all shapes and colours.

All these factors point to the need for a conscious strategy for collecting, conserving and disposing of water.

- Locate drains and sewers on your property. Check under manhole covers and, if necessary, empty a bucket or two of water to determine the direction and destination of the flow. Keep drains clear and working efficiently, and avoid damaging them during any excavation.
- Where possible plan the garden to include areas of exposed soil for rain to penetrate, and lay hard surfaces so that they drain into these beds.
- Intercept rainwater and conserve it for garden use. Water butts tapped into downpipes and larger tanks above or below ground (you may need to install a pump) are convenient and unobtrusive storage containers.
- Alternatively channel rain and surface drainage to garden features such as a pond with a dipping area for watering cans, the reservoir of a flowing water installation or a rain garden.

Make a rain garden

This simple arrangement embeds water management in playful garden features and a specialized planting area. Rainwater is first collected from gutters in a water butt. The surplus is ducted from an overflow directly, or via one or more water devices such as a cascade or bamboo spout, to arrive finally in a bog garden of moisture-loving plants. Any overflow from this is led to a drain. 'Grey' water from household washing and bathing can be similarly recycled by first passing it through a vertical filter tank and then delivering the cleaned supply to the rain garden or a wildlife pond or reed filter bed.

- Fit guttering to sheds, verandas and conservatories to trap extra water for storage; cover any outbuildings or a porch with a green roof (see page 104), which absorbs rain and then releases it gradually via gutters.
- Ensure that you use paving and surfacing materials that allow some rainwater to seep away and restore natural ground levels. This is especially important on heavy soils (clay shrinks after prolonged drying, which is a prime cause of structural subsidence).

FLOORING MATERIALS

Paths and larger paved areas are essentially functional elements in the garden, and the choice of material will be determined primarily by strength, durability and resilience to wear and weathering; cost and ease of laying are other considerations. Practical and visual fitness also need some thought, though: for example, does the preferred material match the character of the buildings and the surrounding area, will it still look appealing in wet or dull weather, and could it influence the rest of your plan by reflecting light or by suggesting valuable contrast or continuity with the adjacent landscape?

Depending on your preferences, your garden could be a low-maintenance paved entertainment area with special beds and containers for plants (right) or a cool green space for plants and turf – here liberally studded with slabs for easy passage (above).

There are several common surfacing materials to choose from:

Paving slabs Deservedly popular because they are widely available, will quickly cover a large area, and are supplied in a range of sizes for creating various patterns. They may be made from natural stone (the most expensive), reconstituted stone, terracotta,

concrete (the cheapest) or even marble for special sites and warm climates. Lay them on sand over a bed of hardcore, and fill joints with sand, pea gravel, stone dust or soil for drainage.

Bricks Warm, richly coloured and adaptable, these need to be frost-proof to prevent crumbling; engineering bricks are best for damp places because they resist slippery algae. They can be laid on the flat or on edge, in circles as well as in linear or herringbone bonds. Stone setts are similar in size and shape, but harder and with a more rounded profile. Lay as for pavers on a bed of sand.

Timber decking Wooden platforms and boardwalks are ideal for uneven ground, patios and other gathering places, and lightweight versions are suitable for balconies and roofs. In wet districts timber may become slippery unless surfaced with wire mesh or textured paint. Supplied as long boards for nailing or screwing to timber bearers or as panels that can be bedded on gravel, decking is made from expensive but durable hardwoods, decay-resistant cedar or pressure-treated softwoods. Check that supplies come from responsibly managed forests and, wherever possible, opt for eco-friendly preservative treatments.

A flight of steps can merely provide access to another level, or it can make a strong contribution to style and atmosphere, as here, where the broad brick treads add a sense of grandeur to the entrance, tempered by nonchalant ground-level plantings and the almost frivolous charm of the standard roses.

Design tips

- Mix materials with care to avoid distracting fussiness. Stone setts surrounded by timber decking and flagstones edged or divided by lines of bricks are attractive combinations.
- All loose aggregates need robust edging to prevent migration on to beds and other adjacent surfaces. Good edge materials include gravel, boards, slates, bricks, flexible lawn edging strips and terracotta tiles.
- For an instant weathered look, explore recycled and salvaged surfacing. Stone slabs and setts will have developed an aged patina, old bricks have a special rustic charm and timber decking will have lost its raw appearance.
- Use modular surfacing like bricks and slabs to reshape the garden space. Aligning bricks across a path makes it look wider; laying them parallel to its sides, especially if the path physically tapers a little as it recedes, increases a sense of distance.

Loose materials A host of decorative and often inexpensive loose aggregates can be used for various surfacing purposes, all of them easy to spread and often contributing exciting textures and colours to the garden floor. Gravel and shingle are stone fragments frequently used for drives and large areas, especially where security is important: gravel is irregular and noisy to walk on, while shingle is finer, more rounded and quieter. Both need raking level periodically, tend to trap leaves, soil and weed seeds, and should be laid on a permeable membrane to ensure good drainage and suppress weeds. Stepping stones could be inserted for easy passage. Stone, glass and metal chippings are fine decorative aggregates for infills, edging and mulching. Shredded bark makes a soft, silent path surface for informal gardens.

STEPS

Easy access to different levels will involve building steps, which should be thoughtfully planned as a design feature rather than added as an uninviting accessory. Wide shallow treads emphasize the important transition between levels and force a slower, more leisurely pace.

Aim for a consistent rise of 8–15cm (3–6in) from step to step, and a tread depth of at least 45cm (18in) for comfort: deep treads and a shallow rise can eliminate the need for a handrail. You may be able to build the steps from the same material as the path or platform they meet,

Subtlety isn't everything, when desiging a garden. An extravagant flourish is sometimes more honest. Here, a hammock's gaudy fabric and almost monumental timber supports proclaim the unashamed pleasure of lazing in the open air.

or prefer a contrast to give them a stronger presence. If you use the garden after dark, remember to arrange some kind of lighting, such as solar-powered beacons at both sides, to prevent accidents.

DRIVES AND CAR PARKS

Access and off-road parking for cars at the front or side of properties is a common and inescapable necessity in cities. An existing hard surface such as concrete or asphalt is difficult and expensive to change, but might make an ideal standing ground for containers and even a collection area for harvesting rainwater (see page 53).

When laying a new parking or access surface, consider using a porous material that will admit rain and so reduce the speed and volume of surface water entering overloaded drainage systems. Gravel and shingle can be spread over a weed-suppressant membrane, which may be punctured in places for direct planting into the soil beneath (finer gravels are easier to maintain and rake level, and supply an attractive background for smaller plants). Perforated bricks and waffle-like pavers can be laid on sand and planted with grass or prostrate flowers like thymes, arenaria, saxifrages and tiny veronicas.

Check if total coverage is really necessary: two wheel-tracks of slabs within a permeable surround of turf or gravel might be sufficient for vehicles, or a sequence of pavers like stepping stones for a pathway.

PLAYGROUND

Family gardens need to cater for children's activity, ideally close to the house. They might require a hard surface for riding or wheeling toys, for example, or a sandpit, which should have a removable cover to keep the contents dry and inaccessible to cats or dogs. In later years the pit could be lined and turned into a pond or planted up as a flower or vegetable bed.

To reduce accidents, avoid hard or rough surfaces in high-impact spaces near swings and similar play equipment: concrete and angular gravel can cause more painful injury than washed sand, round pea-shingle, play bark (less splintery than ordinary shredded bark), plastic matting, or recycled granulated tyres, available in a range of colours.

LAWNS

Mown grass has a genial and inviting appearance, but the size of garden as well as family needs will determine whether a lawn is a feasible or unrealistic proposition. Choose a hard-wearing grass mixture to withstand children's play, or a finer blend for a strictly ornamental lawn.

Planting part of the turf with bulbs or wildflowers can help a lawn work harder in a small garden and reduce the amount of mowing it needs (remember to allocate storage space for a mower and possibly edging shears). Mowing selected areas or pathways in the grass at a different height from the rest can make a lawn look larger and more interesting.

Where space is too restricted for a ground-level lawn, consider making steps, a bank or a seat from turf: keep it trimmed with hedge- or sheep-shears, and speckle part of the feature with small bulbs like crocuses, cyclamen, fritillaries and dwarf narcissi or natural grassland flowers such as primroses and violets.

UTILITY ROOM

No matter how small, a garden has to cater for daily practicalities as well as plants and pleasure, and you might need to find room for a dustbin and recycling containers (including a compost bin), storage for tools or play equipment, and some kind of clothes-drying facility.

You may be able to disperse these in odd corners, although each will then need dry-shod direct access. Otherwise group items together on a hard-surfaced area, near the house and possibly separated from the rest of the garden by plantings or neatly screened from view by fencing that can double as support for plants.

A washing line needs to be accessible from a path for its full length, but small-scale alternatives such as a revolving dryer or a retractable line on a reel or pulley could occupy less room. Tools and toys (or a dustbin) can be housed in a purpose-built lockable store with hinged doors, sides that double as plant supports and a top for use as a table or work surface.

Although essential garden accessories, sheds have traditionally skulked in corners, quite needlessly. The shed can readily be upgraded to provide a canopied sitting place and private office or workshop (left), for example, or a more fanciful chalet, complete with window boxes and shutters (right).

A hardworking shed

Although it might seem an extravagance where space is rationed, a lean-to shed has a relatively small footprint and can be made to earn its keep if used to store fold-up furniture, a mower or bicycle, gardening tools and other portable items. Attach a bench outside in a choice position, fit windows with boxes for plants and train others – whether flowers, fruit or climbing vegetables – up trellis and wires on the walls (and perhaps overhead) to make a small bower. Fix guttering to collect water, and clad the roof with plants (see page 104) to intercept rain and supply camouflage.

Miniature greenhouses occupy very little ground space, even on a balcony, provided the lightweight frame can be secured to a wall. With several shelves inside, one of these could house a good number of seedlings and plants, while standing tall enough to plant with tomatoes and other heat-loving crops in summer.

THE GARDEN BOUNDARIES

Depending on the locality, your garden could have a high, blank brick, concrete or stucco wall on one or more sides, an overgrown and threadbare hedge, or a token new-build line of mesh or wires threaded through concrete posts. Some front gardens are divided by mature fences, hedges and trees, others by nothing more than a strip of soil in a communal landscape.

Before deciding on any alterations your first move should be to find out who owns your boundary – you, or a neighbour, or possibly the ground landlord – and if there are any legal restraints on your making changes. Always communicate and negotiate to avoid blighting relationships with other residents.

Where you can build from new, the choice will be between a fence, wall or hedge, or possibly a combination of any two. A fence is quicker and cheaper to erect than a wall and requires less space and maintenance than a hedge (see page 97). External fences should be sturdy and secure, while structures within a garden or between neighbours could be as lightweight as hazel hurdles or an open picket fence combined with flowering plants or hedging to take over when the fence ends its useful life.

Walls offers privacy and shelter and, although the intial investment is high, as walls are expensive to build, a well-built wall will have a long life and age gracefully. Brick walls suit most urban surroundings unless there is an existing tradition of building with a local material such as stone. If you intend painting the wall or cladding it with plants, lightweight concrete blocks may be acceptable. Make sure foundations are adequate for the height and volume of the wall, and finish off the top with a complementary coping.

Existing walls

Rather than having to start from scratch, you are more likely to inherit existing boundaries in various states of repair. A weak or dilapidated fence can be mended or replaced, while neglected hedges usually respond to hard pruning and some discreet repair.

An old wall in poor condition needs more care. A flaking finish can be wire-brushed off, together with any spalling brick or stone fragments. Chase out crumbling mortar joints to a depth of about 1cm (½in), and repoint with a 5:1 sand/cement mix.

You could then paint the renovated wall, choosing a soft lime-wash white for Mediterranean-style courtyards and sunny sites, pale or neutral shades to introduce extra light, or darker colours if you want drama or to make a far wall recede. Repainting will be needed at regular intervals, the frequency depending on your microclimate. Another option is to coat the wall with a rendering, which can be finished smooth with a plasterer's trowel, roughly by hand in adobe style, or embedded with mosaic glass and china fragments.

Where a wall is quite beyond redemption, camouflage it with an inner fence of trellis, hurdles of bamboo, hazel or willow, or a fence of boards, poles or spaced upright railway sleepers. Lattice frames and wires intended to

Walls may be surfaced or painted, as here, to supply a contrasting background for plants.

Used architecturally, wooden trellis can achieve an almost baroque exuberance that needs no embellishment with plants – especially if it is painted in a complementary colour or combined with a trompe l'oeil mirror for added depth and surprise.

Trellis craft

Although sometimes perceived as a simple support cliché, trellis has a long and inspired history of creative use in the building of airy structures and ornamental follies (treillage), which add height without bulk. The standard wooden form can introduce a pleasantly rustic flavour to urban gardens as well as helping disguise eyesores and supply height. For a more fashionable industrial look, use 15mm copper or chrome tubing and pressure unions to build open, even fanciful structures, either freestanding or attached to walls; drill the pipes for attaching taut wires or coloured nylon rope to make lattice infills.

bear climbing plants need fixing to the wall with galvanized or stainless steel 'vine eyes' screwed at intervals into plugs.

High walls

Excessively tall walls may dominate and crowd the scene, but their impact can be reduced in a number of ways.

Painting a wall up to a height of about 1.5–1.8m (5–6ft) divides its expanse and draws the eye down to garden level. A strip of open lattice panels arranged as a token roof overhead about 2.4m (8ft) high will break up the offending view without excluding light. Do not be tempted to build a screen higher than the garden is wide, though, as this will only reinforce a sense of confinement.

IMPROVING A VIEW

Some features of the urban landscape cannot be altered, in which case you need to resort to concealment, distraction or some other form of guile. Take another look at your surroundings first, though: architecture has its own distinctive beauty, the industrial and distressed looks are both intermittently trendy, and even shabby can be chic. The existing view might have more appeal on reflection than you first thought.

The garden within

Examine the garden from the house, from any upstairs windows as well as the doorway – this is the dominant view – and watch where your eye wanders. If it strays immediately to boundaries that lack interest or charm, plan improvements there, by disguising them with lavish planting and other embellishments to make the garden more inward-looking.

Try adding sculpture, found objects, an extravagant water feature or arrangements of memorabilia, rocks or machinery to keep the focus within. Position the largest in the foreground to grab the attention, with smaller items beyond to distort the normal sense of perspective. Reinforce this effect with boundary wall decoration that harmonizes with the garden contents: bird boxes, a collection of personal treasures, mosaic designs echoed in paving patterns.

Nature is full of bizarre shapes and structures, so sculpture often fits effortlessly into the outdoor scene. It's worth trying anything from an airy geometrical cage (left) made from bent wire (try using recycled hanging baskets) to a more elaborate figure finished in bright mosaic (right).

Using mirrors

A shrewdly placed mirror can magnify space by reflecting part of the garden and suggesting it is larger than in reality. Although an unashamedly theatrical device, this can have a startling effect if you follow simple guidelines.

- Avoid positions at the end of paths, where any hint of a world beyond will be dispelled by the image of you approaching.
- Key sites include boundary walls to suggest an entrance to a secret garden room, or at the far side of a pond to double its perceived surface area.
- Make sure the mirror displays a general part of the garden: reflecting a prominent urn, statue or similarly significant feature can destroy credibility.
- Disguise the edges of a mirror with trellis, a false door- or window-frame, or evergreen foliage to complete the illusion.
- Combine mirrors or mirror tiles with glass brick steps and divisions to reflect more light into gloomy passageways and stairwells.
- Keep the mirrors clean for convincing results!

Garden mirrors are often tucked seamlessly in place to deceive the eye, but an alternative and more direct approach is to hang it like a painting on a wall, to make a framed picture that reflects a particularly satisfying view or composition.

Add plants that climb from ground-level beds or tumble from wall pots and baskets, and vary the height of those growing near the wall so that they confuse the eyeline and draw attention from the margins back to your garden.

Beyond the boundary

Structures and features outside the garden may be beyond practical alteration or improvement, but you can still edit your view of them by emphasizing or concealing their prominence in the landscape.

A neighbour's tree or climber overhanging your garden can legally be thinned or pruned back to the boundary wall or fence (it is politic to discuss plans first, though, and in return make sure your plants do not intrude on next door's space or over a public right of way). Plants beyond your boundary that appeal to you as part of the scene may be worth 'borrowing' visually, allowing them to be part of the overall garden scheme.

Obscure an eyesore by planting a tree or tall shrub in the way, or by increasing the boundary height if this is permitted. Altering the full length of a wall is rarely necessary, and a strategically placed gable end or mock battlement of trellis may offer adequate concealment. Installing a rival feature like a mural, planted arbour or pergola in the same line of vision could distract attention sufficiently, but remember to match the style and scale of

This sitting space is designed as a room within a room, defined by its own frame of hedging and separated from the open garden by a froth of lady's mantle (*Alchemilla mollis*) and an immaculate stockade of young trees whose branches could later be pleached – woven together – to form an aerial hedge.

The structural plan in this garden emphasizes geometry and height, rising from the classic topiary box spheres and yew spirals to the decorative hedge buttresses and tall clean-boled trees pruned to form an arched gateway over the entrance to the dining area.

flamboyant foliage against stark architectural angles. Tiered planting around the sides can produce a lush bank of foliage, hiding boundaries and fostering intimacy: include graceful arching plants like maples, birch and crab apples to embroider the overhead view.

the rest of the garden or else you might replace a monstrosity with a visual howler.

If your plans for your garden are likely to block an attractive scene, consider moving proposed features to one or both sides, to frame rather than obscure the view. An opening could be made in the boundary to display an appealing scene beyond, perhaps by artfully shaping the gap as a revealing window in a topiary hedge or constructing a circular timber 'moon gate' framework in a fence or wall. In a small garden any appealing feature from beyond is worth considering for inclusion to help expand the variety of interest and create a bond with the wider landscape.

If you are overlooked, consider stretching strong wires from side to side above head height, and train lightly foliaged deciduous plants like grapes and kiwi fruit for privacy and dappled shade in summer (and almost full light in winter). On a rooftop a canopy of pergola timbers could supply a reassuring sense of enclosure.

Use any overhead structure for lighting effects such as candle lanterns, coloured spotlights or strings of fairy lights, and other accessories like wind chimes or bird feeders. Suspend panels of clear polycarbonate or open-weave textiles to filter wind or screen a small special place.

PLANNING FOR HEIGHT

Exploiting the vertical dimension can liberate you from the constraints of finite ground space, offering extra growing capacity, a roomier sense of enclosure and privacy, and a visual link between floor and sky. The options are many. Deploy a few oversize shrubs or trees, in tubs if necessary, to defy the garden's scale, and contrast

If you also occupy the floor above, link the two by training tall plants up wall wires – a pear fan or a vigorous climbing rose, for example. Install matching window boxes planted with exuberant trailers for a hanging curtain effect.

Turn a passageway into a leafy tunnel with overhead supports or arches, and clothe these with trained wisteria or laburnum: this will filter wind, alter the scale of a narrow gap between tall buildings, and transform a functional access route into a welcoming entrance and avenue.

INTRODUCING WATER

Still or moving water adds a magical atmosphere to any garden, but can be a particularly powerful and soothing influence in urban surroundings, which often seem oppressively hot, dry or dusty. Throughout their long history town gardens have included reflective pools of water to mirror the shapes and patterns of walls, buildings and sky, and as an aid to tranquil reflection. Tumbling or bubbling water will cool and refresh the air as well as delight the senses with its sparkling vivacity and animated sounds that can soften or even mask intrusive noise from outside. Remember that children find water totally irresistible, and that just a few centimetres depth can be lethal.

Pools of water

A pool may be anything from a generous wildlife pond, stocked with native plants and tucked away safe from disturbance, to a small bowl on a balcony to attract birds or embellish with flower heads and floating candles. More ambitious designs might include still water in shallow channels, troughs or canals across the garden or as a

The hard insistent outlines of the built structures collaborate at night with the soft fluid leaf shapes and pools of still water in a stimulating counterpoint of lights and reflections.

moat round a patio, perhaps illuminated by submerged uplighters. You could even build the whole garden design around a large shallow area of water, perhaps bearing large floating planters of marginal and bog plants.

Moving water

Adding a circulating pump to your design allows you to install a fountain, waterfall, geyser or trickling wall plaque or bamboo spout, as a focal point or a major participant in the living garden. You should match the size of pump to the volume of water that requires moving, although this need not be great: just a drizzle or film of water can animate its surroundings. Make sure mains electricity is installed and maintained by a qualified electrician, or use solar-powered and low-voltage devices. Instead of deliberately propelling water, you could reroute rainwater as an intermittent flowing feature, ducted along channels, down chains or through pipes, and perhaps emerging eventually in a pond or small rain garden (see page 53).

ADDING LIGHTING

Artificial lighting can alter the garden setting and atmosphere dramatically, introducing a mysterious gleam or striking highlights to the surroundings or allowing you to enjoy the garden after sunset. All outdoor lighting should be used with discretion, however: a subtle glow can be more satisfying than bright floodlighting, using less energy and making a smaller contribution to already excessive urban light pollution.

These stone spheres have a comfortable organic shape that is captivating both as bubble fountains in a ribbon of loose aggregates (opposite) and as companion sculpture for dramatic leaf forms, especially when illuminated at night to create a harmony of shapes and shadows (left).

For total freedom and security, wild creatures prefer cover at all levels while foraging and feeding. This garden offers both tree protection from overhead predators and the comfort of the damp darkness behind containers.

Make sure you distinguish between primary lighting, designed to illuminate areas, passageways and entrances to ensure safety and security, and secondary lighting, which is installed for aesthetic or playful effect, to supply ambience or diversity to the darkened garden. Devices may be solar powered, storing energy by day and then often switching on automatically at dusk, or low voltage and connected to the mains via a transformer. As with water features, make sure any mains supply is professionally installed, with weatherproof fittings.

URBAN WILDLIFE

Cities might not seem obviously appealing habitats for wild things, but a host of birds, mammals and invertebrates are very much at home there, often thanks to our gardening activities. Some arrive as refugees from habitat loss or pesticide use in the surrounding countryside; others may be top predators such as foxes and hawks, opportunists that follow the supply of food.

Railway embankments, canal towpaths, tree-lined streets and road verges offer corridors for safe movement deep into towns and connect gardens like a string of pearls. Taken en masse these green oases may comprise a nation's biggest nature reserve.

Your garden will almost certainly be visited by birds, especially where nearby trees, hedges or large shrubs conceal their wary approach. Other flying visitors may include dragonflies, bumblebees, water beetles, butterflies and moths; owls and bats will inspect your garden for prey at night. Small mammals such as mice, voles and shrews may be found at ground level, together with toads, frogs and newts in damp gardens. The soil itself can host a huge population of secretive insects and other tiny creatures, some of them rare or endangered.

Encouraging wildlife

You may not have room for a woodland, wetland or wildflower meadow, but the simplest invitation can yield unexpected results: a wink is as good as a nod where nature is concerned. A few pelargoniums or impatiens in summer can entice hummingbird hawk moths; a dish of clean water on a table or at the end of a window box can satisfy thirsty birds in dry or frozen weather; and a modest pile of autumn leaves will often attract resting invertebrates or a foraging hedgehog.

To encourage wildlife, start by relaxing the way you maintain the garden: zealous tidiness is a human failing and rarely benefits flora or fauna. A little judicious decay, for example, can yield dividends because decomposition involves micro-organisms that feed larger creatures. Recycle plant waste in a compost heap, which can become a favourite haunt of toads, shrews and countless wriggly mini-beasts, and then spread the product as a nutritious mulch for robins, thrushes and blackbirds to ransack.

Gather fallen tree leaves in a heap to rot down, in the process turning into a miniature nature reserve that offers winter sanctuary for many creatures. Leave seedheads for hungry finches, or tidy them into an accessible bundle out of the way. Above all give up the routine use of chemical pesticides and fungicides, most of which kill friend and foe alike and destroy the food supply of the wildlife you aim to attract.

Creating mini-habitats

The next step is to offer tempting places for creatures to feed, breed or rest.

- Pile prunings or rotting logs in a corner for wood-borers like beetles, wood wasps and ichneumon flies.
- A heap of stones and soil will attract ground bees, mice, wrens, mosses and trailing wildflowers.
- Grow plants close together to create dark cover for ground-feeding birds and nocturnal mammals.
- Plant climbers on walls and fences to provide nesting and foraging sites safe from prowling cats and other urban predators.
- Hang out feeders filled with nuts, seeds and fatty foods for different kinds of birds.

In this wildlife-friendly garden simple corridors of continuous foliage provide cover that allows creatures to travel safely along the ground.

- Install nest boxes in safe places, ideally during autumn so that birds can explore them as roosts before the breeding season.
- Make a pond or still water feature for toads, newts and numerous aquatic insects.

Seductive flowers

Butterflies and bees can be enticed to your garden if you plant flowers that produce plenty of nectar and pollen. Outstanding examples include agrostemma, *Buddleja davidii* cultivars, caryopteris, ceanothus, cornflower (*Centaurea cyanus*), crocus species, hebe, heliotrope, hyssop, lavender, honeysuckle (especially *Lonicera periclymenum*), saponaria, sedum, thyme, *Verbena bonariensis* and *Viburnum tinus*.

3

PLANTING CITY GARDENS

A garden means different things to different people – an outdoor space for idling and pottering, a son et lumière composition of light and water or somewhere for a children's trampoline, for example – but to many it immediately suggests growing plants. Even the most austere contemporary space can gain style and character from a few imposing specimens, arranged as one would choice houseplants indoors. The majority of familiar garden species will thrive in a city habitat, together with many others that may positively relish the protected conditions it provides.

Choosing plants to populate your garden is an opportunity to indulge in your favourite flowers – you might have a passion for roses (always content in the clay typical of so many urban plots), for example, or prefer a merry mix of all sorts in an informal arrangement that almost defiantly installs nature in an urban context.

MAKING A START WITH PLANTS

How you set about introducing plants depends on a number of practical factors, such as the time of year, the stage of progress of any preliminary work or hard landscaping, and whether the garden is already established or a clear site.

Strategies

Before introducing plants, pause to consider how to go about it. There are many excellent garden designers who specialize in urban gardens, and can both supply plans and organize the work. If you are not confident of your own ideas, it may be better to share them with a planner who can translate them into a working plan.

Perhaps you have seen a total scheme you like, in a book or during a garden visit – many large gardens open to the public contain inspired corners capable of imitation at home – and would like to adapt this for your own garden, to create yourself in your own time. Or you might prefer to develop one small area at a time, feeling your way and including odd plants as you discover them and find that they thrive.

Each approach is valid, but you need to decide early on which feels most comfortable and fits in with other demands on your time and energy.

Any bare-root plants are best introduced in autumn or while dormant, because spring and summer planting can entail more attention to watering, especially in a hot dry season. Mid-season planting may be unavoidable, however, especially with some vegetables at a critical stage in their life cycle. Container-grown stock can be planted at any time in theory, although the same caution about post-planting care applies; plants to grow in containers can be introduced at any time.

Before planting, allow alterations to structures and terrain to settle down, especially if you have treated wood with

Growing plants in pots compensates for inadequate or nonexistent soil and extends the potential of available ground: exploit this decorative opportunity to its utmost by reserving front-row positions for distinguished or dramatic plants such as hostas (left), rodgersias, rhubarb, ferns or grasses (right), all displayed in your very best containers.

Above all, don't be impatient. The best gardens are the result of evolution, not revolution. Instant gardens are usually banal, rarely look perfect for long, and make little provision for change as plants and tastes develop. A garden is essentially a society of plants, and like all successful communities needs time to interact and mature.

REVIVING AN OVERGROWN GARDEN

At first sight clearing or rejuvenating a neglected garden can seem daunting but, as with any major overhaul, the secret of success is to advance in carefully planned, manageable stages.

First clear obvious debris, rubble and dumped rubbish, for salvage or disposal (see page 41). Possibly more will come to light as you disturb the soil or a long-standing tangle of undergrowth.

Decide whether trees are to be removed or revived. Many species tolerate being cut back hard, even coppiced down to stumps, and respond with vigorous young growth for thinning or pruning to a pleasing shape later.

preservatives, or imported or deeply disturbed the soil – this needs several weeks to consolidate and hold adequate water for any length of time.

Tread gently when clearing or cutting back established plants, and if in doubt postpone irreversible changes, for up to a year ideally, until you are certain what you have. Existing gardens may hold surprises: an unidentified nondescript shrub could suddenly redeem itself with blossom, an overgrown corner might host wildlife such as newts, toads or even snakes, and buried bulbs can spring into life in almost any season.

Conifers rarely stand cutting back hard, however, but can be topped or shaped to admit more light (see page 31). Complete removal of a mature tree may mean employing a specialist or you might be able to saw it down in manageable portions yourself – cut the prunings into small pieces to stack out of the way as a beetle or small mammal refuge.

Most shrubs and hedges can be restored by hard pruning. Remove the oldest stems of shrubs and shorten younger growth; trim overgrown hedges in stages, first the side and then the top the following year. Again conifers can be reluctant to respond, but any reduction in height of common hedging species such as the notorious but immensely valuable x *Cupressocyparis leylandii* will be disguised after a few years by soft new lateral growth. If you need to take out a large shrub or hedge completely, first saw or chop down most of the topgrowth, leaving just enough stems for leverage, and then use a mattock rather than a spade to excavate the roots.

Overgrown herbaceous plants may be worth keeping if they are healthy, in which case lift clumps with a fork, split them into segments with a spade and replant younger pieces in new homes. Any to discard altogether can be lifted complete; shake off the soil and stack the bare roots to rot. Cut down perennial weeds with shears, a strimmer or a sickle, and add to the

Cunningly hidden supports leave shelves of decking apparently floating in tiers up to a raised platform set amidst a group of palms, nearly hardy Japanese bananas (*Musa basjoo*) and similar subtropical species to create an exotic corner suntrap.

compost heap. Fork out the roots, teasing out as many fragments as possible, and discard these because they often regrow in a compost heap, unless you first dry them in the sun until brittle enough to compost safely or soak them in a bucket of water to make liquid fertilizer.

Another (slower) option is to cut or mow weed growth to the ground and then cover the area with black plastic sheeting for a year to kill the roots (ground elder and bindweed roots may take two years). Weeds in paving will eventually succumb if you persistently cut off any regrowth; otherwise spot-treat them carefully with a systemic herbicide such as glyphosate.

If you want to remove turf, use a spade to chop the area into rows of small rectangles and then lift these turves and stack like bricks. You could build raised beds or containers for wildflowers with them, or simply stockpile them neatly and cover with black plastic until they rot into fibrous material for returning to the soil after a year or two, in which case cut holes in the top of the sheet to plant sweet peas or squashes for a decorative disguise in the meantime.

CHOOSING A STYLE

Even when allowances are made for environmental constraints such as shade or lack of light, there is a wealth of desirable plants to explore for city gardens of all kinds. Whatever the size of plot, every gardener has to be selective, however, and this is particularly true where space is at a premium.

Decide on general principles first: whether to grow flowers or food crops, for example, or to aim for an anarchic cottage-style medley or a calm arrangement of formal specimens. Do you have a strong preference for permanent low-maintenance perennials, or a cheerful but labour-intensive sequence of brilliant seasonal bedding, or an easy-going mixture of all kinds?

A small enclosed site can be perfect for creating a particular theme or international style. You might perhaps opt for a typical Japanese courtyard, blending natural features such as rocks, water, small trees, ferns and mosses to assemble a miniature landscape on a balcony or cool shady patio. A minimalist theme using innovative paving materials, strategic lighting and sculptural plants often looks effective in stark industrial surroundings.

Many exotic and subtropical plants revel in a sunny warm urban backyard, as do Mediterranean plants such as olives, rosemaries, pistacia, felicia, amaryllis and crinum lilies; even summer bedding plants like pelargoniums and fuchsias will often stay healthy and virtually evergreen in sheltered gardens.

Remember that your plants have to compete with any other activities you plan for your garden – they might need to be robust if a ball is being kicked about, for example – and will require a certain amount of basic care and maintenance, especially in a dry summer when you might want to be away for several weeks, or a harsh winter when you would rather stay indoors. You will also need to match planting plans with the local microclimate, allowing for high rainfall, spasmodic risk of frost or summer drought perhaps, and for the garden's prevailing aspect, its depth and duration of shade, and exposure to wind.

If you are new to gardening, choose easy and inexpensive varieties until you feel confident enough to try more temperamental or sensitive urban favourites like bananas and tree ferns.

A perfumed garden
Pervading fragrance might seem an appealing urban daydream, especially in a context of tainted street air, and there are many lovely scented flowers you could include in any scheme, but beware of excess. When designing a sensory garden it is easy to make the mistake of

An irresistible midsummer show of climbing roses throngs a sweeping arch of tubular steel, enclosing the paved area like a perfumed arbour; on the bench containers of mixed pelargoniums await dispersal round the sunlit yard.

including a multitude of fragrances that ultimately clash or cancel each other, whereas just a sprinkling of sweet alyssum (*Lobularia maritima*) in crevices between sun-baked pavers is often enough to fill the still evening air in a small garden with their scent of fresh honey. Choose a few favourites and make sure they are compatible or space them well apart (especially powerful kinds like *Lilium regale* or *Nicotiana alata*); for maximum indulgence position them under a window, beside a seat or where you pass near by.

Some plants share their perfume only when touched or at close quarters, but others can stir the senses at a distance in the slightest breeze. Notable among these are wallflowers (*Erysimum cheiri*), wintersweet (*Chimonanthus praecox*), *Daphne odora*, crown imperial (*Fritillaria imperialis*), *Iris germanica*, shrubby philadelphus, most jasmines and honeysuckles, hyacinths, old-fashioned roses, stocks (forms of *Matthiola*), lilac (*Syringa*), mahonias and lily of the valley.

PLACES TO GROW PLANTS

An established garden will probably offer a host of sites for the introduction of new plants.

A garden on a new-build site may be a recently levelled expanse of topsoil that should be left for several months to settle and will almost certainly benefit from some kind of improvement (see page 94) wherever you allocate plants. A site that has been turfed could be marked out immediately with a plan of flower or vegetable beds: mow the lawn until you are ready to start, and compost the mowings to add to your new beds.

A paved yard can be adapted for growing plants by lifting one or more pavers, removing any sand or concrete bedding and then cultivating the exposed soil. If you have a concrete or tarmac surface, treat the garden as a patio and build raised beds, at least 30cm (12in) deep but no more than about 1m (39in) high for comfort. Pressure-treated timber, railway sleepers, bricks, stone and precast concrete are all suitable for the walls, but make sure there are plenty of seep holes along the base for drainage and channel this water safely away to a drain or separate water feature.

Using containers

The most flexible arrangement for soil-less gardens and rooftops (and the *only* option for most balconies) is to grow plants in containers. There is a huge selection of available sizes and styles of containers in a range of materials, or you could improvise with any kind of receptacle, from paint tins to plastic-lined baskets, provided it drains efficiently at the base. Pots and containers are often handsome artefacts, and in small gardens could be selected as sculptural assets in their own right, combining function with form.

Choose the largest practicable size to reduce watering needs, and mulch the surface with a decorative material such as bark, glass beads or scraps of rock and slate to conserve moisture and lift a utilitarian appearance.

Plunging small pot plants to their rims in a larger container of soil or compost makes them easier to tend in hot, windy or frosty conditions, and their massed appearance contributes to their impact. Remember that full, moist containers are heavy, so avoid overloading balconies and roofs; if you need to move larger plants under cover in winter or into more sunlight at other times

Containers of various natural materials like stone, clay and slatted wood jostle with cheerfully painted neighbours and house a range of easy-going plants, from perennials like cordylines and box topiary to seasonal highlights such as late spring violas and tulips (opposite), or the headily fragrant midsummer trumpets of *Lilium longiflorum* (below).

93

Plants for shade

Insufficient sunlight affects plants in different ways: many variegated cultivars turn green and lose much of their distinctive colouring, while others simply refuse to flower or can grow unusually tall and weak in their quest for light. About six hours' sunshine daily is often a critical threshold, while indirect light from the side can redeem some darker spots. Experiment with crocuses, snowdrops, cyclamen, soleirolia, *Erigeron karvinskianus*, *Mentha requienii* and *Oxalis triangularis* at low level, and with begonias and impatiens in summer. Mid-height plants might include aubrieta, campanula, dicentra, hosta, hydrangea, monarda, phlox, polygonatum, primula, pulmonaria, schizostylis, tradescantia and tricyrtis. On shaded walls try *Akebia quinata*, *Cotoneaster horizontalis*, *Jasminum nudiflorum* and roses such as 'Gloire de Dijon', 'Madame Alfred Carrière' and 'Mermaid'.

of year, fit the base of the containers with castors or stand them on wheeled trolleys.

IMPROVING YOUR SOIL

Gardeners routinely feed plants when growth falters or shows signs of distress, but the long-term vitality of any garden depends more on regularly feeding the soil with organic matter such as manure or compost.

Healthy soil contains huge numbers of microscopic

To make the most of a small city plot the gardener may need to be both artist and artisan. Here the soil has been improved until it can support a lush population of ferns, grasses, bamboos and bold foliage plants, whose distinctive shapes are then blended together to furnish an imaginative landscape.

organisms which turn these waste materials into humus, the fibrous and spongy substance that gives topsoil its dark colour, adds fertility and amends soil structure. Humus levels need topping up annually as the raw material breaks down into minerals and nutrients, a process that usually accelerates in warmer seasons and regions.

As well as adding fertility, humus improves the quality of almost every kind of soil: it opens up sticky clay, making it more workable and free-draining, and fortifies light soils by trapping moisture and binding their loose sandy grains into larger crumbs. Neglected town soil is often dry and dusty primarily because its humus content is minimal or nonexistent.

It may also smell sour when disturbed. This is a sign of acidity: the heavy rainfall prevalent over many cities washes out soluble calcium, turning the soil progressively more acid. This may not be a problem if you want to grow rhododendrons, blueberries, heathers and other acid-loving species, but many plants (especially vegetables) prefer neutral or slightly alkaline soils, which means adding garden lime during cultivation. A simple soil-testing kit from a garden centre will

measure your soil's acidity level and indicate how much lime to add (the liberal use of dried, crushed eggshells to ward slugs off plants can also sustain calcium levels).

If the soil is shallow or drains slowly, you could avoid laborious earthworks by building raised beds and filling these with good-quality topsoil, which can often be bought or delivered in convenient bags. This extra depth encourages strong roots and greater moisture retention in drought as well as improved drainage of surplus rainfall.

Finding fertility

As they grow, plants gradually consume nutrients stored in the soil, so you need to replace these regularly to maintain vigorous and healthy growth. Chemical fertilizers will supply a plant's basic nutritional requirements, but they provide nothing of lasting benefit, their long-term use is often the cause of poor soil texture and structure in urban gardens, and their manufacture can consume a lot of energy or cause environmental problems.

Many gardeners prefer to use organic materials such as seaweed-based fertilizers for container plants and compost or manure for the ground, because they condition and improve soil as well as feeding growth. The main problem for town gardeners is sourcing adequate supplies of these bulky materials. Bags of processed manures or compost are convenient to handle but may be costly, especially in quantity.

The best solution is to make as much of your own compost as possible. Local authorities often supply inexpensive composters to process kitchen and plant waste. Bulk up this soft material with fibrous waste like torn-up newspaper and card, floor sweepings, vacuum-cleaner contents and tree leaves, but aim for a roughly equal balance between these 'brown' or carbon-rich fibrous materials and the soft 'green' nitrogenous ingredients.

If you are short of space or only produce small but regular amounts of compostable waste, consider using a wormery instead. This is a compact insulated chamber in which thousands of compost worms steadily transform added ingredients into friable worm casts for topdressing or potting plants, plus a potent nutritious liquid for

Sometimes simplicity is the most restful option: here, an evergreen photinia hedge for shelter, a bank of multiflora petunias and a choice potted fan palm are all it takes to create a pleasing uncluttered setting for dining in the evening sunlight.

supplementary feeding. Share these products selectively around your plants for maximum value.

Additional organic supplies

- Neighbours and friends may keep rabbits, chickens or pigeons, all sources of concentrated fertilizer. They might also donate lawn mowings to mix with torn-up newspapers for making a fast and bulky compost.
- Straw and hay bedding (but not wood shavings) from domestic pets rots down quickly if mixed with green materials like nettles or grass clippings.
- Urine is a traditional fertilizer high in nitrogen, and can be used to enrich compost and speed up its decomposition.
- Gather fallen leaves in your street: they are free, annually renewed and usually unwanted. Stored in a wire-netting enclosure or perforated black bin-liners, they will rot slowly into a pleasant soil improver and mulch material.
- Grow a green manure in any empty ground to fork in later as a soil conditioner: crimson clover, blue phacelia, annual lupins and buckwheat are all productive and popular with bees and hoverflies.

- Explore your locality for compost ingredients: market stalls, greengrocers and restaurants are often happy to donate discarded vegetables and trimmings.
- 'Never come home empty-handed' is a sound country saying. Take a bag wherever you go and collect tree leaves, nettles, molehill soil, farm animal droppings or dead bracken (high in potash).
- Save naturally acid coffee grounds and tea leaves for topdressing and mulching ericaceous (acid-loving) plants in containers and the open ground; spent teabags can be used in the bottom of pots to cover drainage holes.

URBAN HEDGES

Gardeners tend to view hedges with mixed feelings. A hedge will occupy more ground – up to a metre in width – than a fence or wall, takes several years to establish, and requires clipping or pruning to shape at least once a year, a formal disciplined hedge several times.

On the other hand it is a more durable, less expensive and often more visually satisfying option, offering a safe corridor for birds to move around their territory and providing the garden with effective weather protection by gently filtering rather than confronting strong wind.

Depending on the type of plants used, a hedge may act as a dense, glossy evergreen boundary, an informal background to a collection of herbaceous plants, or a colourful feature in its own right if you choose species with bright flowers or fruits. You can even make a live mobile screen for occasional privacy by growing a row of dense evergreens like box, hebe or yew in a long narrow plant trough fitted with castors.

When starting a hedge, do not source large quantities of hedging plants from a garden centre: specimens are usually too large, which means they take much longer to establish, and more expensive than small young stock bought in bulk from a specialist nursery. After planting cut all plants except conifers back to half their height to encourage solid bushy growth.

Hedging plants for city gardens

In bleak or polluted areas choose from beech, *Cotoneaster simonsii*, deutzia, *Euonymus japonicus* cultivars, hazel, holly, hornbeam, *Lonicera nitida*, privet, *Prunus cerasifera*, snowberry, spiraea or weigela.

For warm, benign situations you could add box, berberis, ceanothus, cotinus, escallonia, hydrangea, lavender, laurel, *Potentilla fruticosa*, pyracantha, rosemary, rugosa roses, santolina and *Viburnum tinus*.

INCLUDING TREES

There is a lot of merit and deep satisfaction to be derived from planting trees in the city landscape. Apart from any intrinsic beauty their flowers, fruits, foliage or form might have, carefully selected specimen trees can provide varying amounts of local shade, add height and maturity to low-level plantings, disguise an eyesore or frame a view. They help create a false perspective of distance or size, introduce a mood of quiet formality or beguiling nonchalance according to variety and will often tempt birds that would not otherwise visit feeders where there is no overhead cover.

Edible hedges

Where there is space, turn a hedge or screen into a productive feature by planting fruit crops, or introduce a few into an existing mixed hedge. A row of raspberries makes an excellent summer screen; gooseberries can be clipped to a formal shape and blend well with rugosa roses; blueberries thrive and crop heavily on acid soils; and thornless or cut-leaved blackberries and hybrid berries can transform wire netting into an ornamental and economic windbreak. Interplant with damsons, quinces, crab apples or almonds every 3–4m (10–13ft) as small trees to relieve a uniform hedge top.

Wooden joinery, bamboo screens, shaped evergreens and specimen bonsai combine to provide a typically oriental setting for an urban lifestyle.

Acers of all kinds suit city gardens, especially the restrained growth and exquisite leaf shapes of Japanese maples like the various *A. japonicum* and *A. palmatum* cultivars. Plant them freely and watch their foliage catch fire with vivid autumn tints at the season's end.

Tree shapes vary considerably – rounded, towering, slim, weeping or nearly prostrate, for example – and the huge range can offer a form or silhouette to suit every purpose and position, especially in contrast to the rigid lines and angles of buildings. They may be evergreen (which includes most conifers), keeping their leaves permanently but shedding a few of the oldest throughout the year, or deciduous, losing all their foliage in autumn and admitting more light in winter as well as presenting an often fascinating tracery of bare branches.

An urban mini-forest

A proven way to pack a lot of plants into a small space is to imitate the natural layered structure of a woodland ecosystem, where plants occupy a series of tiers in a compatible community. The highest is a canopy of deciduous trees, pruned to admit plenty of light to the plants below. These include a shrub layer, surrounded or underplanted with a ground-level selection of shade-tolerant perennials, plus some climbers that filter their way through to the tree layer. This high-density but amicable arrangement works for both ornamental plants and a mix of perennial vegetable, herb and fruit crops.

Their disadvantages are few. Their roots extend at least as wide as the canopy of topgrowth, possibly competing unfairly against other plants for water and nutrients. More vigorous species may penetrate drains, undermine house foundations or wander into neighbouring gardens if planted too close to buildings and boundaries. Falling leaves, although a free and renewable compost resource, may be a nuisance in ponds and on gravel surfaces. Some of the most desirable species and cultivars are expensive and sometimes slow to grow to significant size. But on balance their inclusion in city gardens is to be encouraged.

Choices for city sites

Research a potential tree type thoroughly before buying. As a major component of any garden plan the ideal candidate will need to satisfy a variety of criteria, and as a long-lived and permanent resident could resent being moved if planted in the wrong place. However, many kinds will grow satisfactorily in a large container or tub for a number of years, at least while you decide on the perfect place for it. When you do plant in the open ground, prepare the site deeply and thoroughly, stake tall kinds for the first two or three years, and allow each a patch of open soil at least 1m (39in) across in any paved area.

Always check potential height and spread, and whether growth will withstand pruning to maintain an acceptable size. Appearances at a garden centre can be deceptive: *Abies balsamea* Hudsonia Group and *Cedrus atlantica*

Glauca Group, for example, are both popular and appealing conifers while young and compact, but the former will reach only 1m (39in), whereas the blue cedar needs masses of space for its ultimate height of 36m (120ft).

Elite trees of moderate size include Korean fir (*Abies koreana*), paperbark maple (*Acer griseum*), snowy mespilus (*Amelanchier lamarckii*), weeping birch (*Betula pendula* 'Youngii'), Judas tree (*Cercis siliquastrum*), goldenrain tree (*Koelreuteria paniculata*), golden rain (*Laburnum* x *watereri* 'Vossii'), Japanese white pine (*Pinus parviflora*, the 'willow pattern' tree), weeping willow-leaved pear (*Pyrus salicifolia* var. *orientalis* 'Pendula'), false acacia (*Robinia pseudoacacia* 'Frisia'), golden Irish yew (*Taxus baccata* 'Fastigiata Aureomarginata'), and numerous crab apple, flowering cherry, hawthorn and rowan cultivars.

For fruit consider apples, apricots, cherries, elderberries, mulberries, peaches, plums and quinces, all on dwarfing stock or trained up a wall. Birches and rowans look particularly attractive if several are planted together in a close cluster to produce a multi-stemmed highlight.

GARDEN PRODUCE

In city gardens around the world growing food is often the top priority – in rooftop allotments on St Petersburg buildings (including the prison), for example, or in Havana, where flat roofs sport rows of lorry-tyre containers packed with peppers and tomatoes. Wherever you are, growing

Whether snipped as a garnish or added to food as a major ingredient, herbs should be close at hand for instant availability. Most flourish happily in pots by the door, but grow more vigorously in deep window boxes, where parsley, for example, will achieve quite robust proportions.

some of your own food is feasible even in tiny gardens, and no harder than growing flowers. The results will be fresh and flavoursome, especially when gathered just before use.

A large back garden could be turned over entirely to self-sufficiency, or you might prefer to allocate a smaller area, ideally near the house for ease of harvest and regular attention. Where space is limited you need to be very selective, confining choices to a few favourites or those crops that benefit most from being fresh – salads and herbs, for example. Some of these are smaller, fast-growing crops that are ideal for containers, window boxes and even hanging baskets.

It is best not to grow vegetables in front gardens. Although exposed to less lead and other toxic substances than a few decades ago, the soil in roadside gardens may still contain a legacy of contaminants that could be absorbed by plants.

To get the most from your plants, choose decorative kinds such as purple peas, asparagus for cutting and

Crops that earn their keep

- Blueberries thrive in large pots of acid compost and are easily protected there from birds; they turn gorgeous shades of red in autumn.
- Carrots in containers at least 45–50cm (18–20in) deep usually escape carrot fly havoc, look decorative and emerge long, straight and clean.
- Runner beans make a colourful and productive summer porch when growing up tall canes either side of a doorway.
- Grapes can be trained on taut overhead wires for light shade, privacy and fresh desserts while you are dining outdoors in late summer.
- Crops like cucumbers, tall peas and beans that will climb poles or trellis save space and conceal an ugly wall or screen a view.
- Grow tumbling tomatoes and parsley together in baskets or boxes for colour, attractive foliage and easy harvest.
- Figs fruit best with confined roots, so grow a fig tree in a container and train the lush, handsome foliage on wires to make a green wall.

Covering roofs with living plants benefits buildings, people and wildlife alike, but varieties need careful selection for tolerance of extreme conditions like wind exposure, drought and high light intensity. Suitable grasses include *Festuca*, *Briza* and *Koeleria* species, plus *Carex* sedges.

flower arrangements, clumps of rhubarb beside a still pool, or scarlet-podded asparagus peas as ground cover. Golden courgettes in a rich blue bin or rainbow chard in glazed pots add startling splashes of unexpected colour. Unusual crops rarely found fresh in shops are also worth growing – whitecurrants, alpine strawberries, seakale or giant garlic, for example.

GREENING BUILDINGS

A growing trend in modern urban design is to use plants as an insulating and decorative surfacing for roofs and walls. The amenity and environmental benefits are various: roof life is extended because the roof absorbs less heat; the heat loss from indoors through walls and roofs is reduced; complex airflows around foliage can cool the immediate atmosphere in summer; the plants intercept considerable amounts of airborne dust particles; and biodiversity improves with the increase in nesting, feeding and hibernating niches.

A robust roof structure is essential for such a scheme because of the weight of the growing materials (substrate), especially when moist. This can add an extra

70–970kg per sq metre (14–200lb per sq ft), depending on its depth: a simple cover of sedums and mosses can thrive in a lightweight layer just 2cm (¾in) deep, whereas herbaceous wildflowers need as much as 15cm (6in) of substrate. New buildings are designed to cope with such weights, but existing roofs could need substantial reinforcement.

For many urban residents greening is a more practical option for a porch, shed, veranda, storage unit or even ledges and parapets than the roof of a house: the plants and substrate protect the fabric of such structures without too much alteration, as well as controlling rainwater movement and generally enhancing appearances. Pre-sown vegetation mats make construction easy, using a suite of undemanding flowering species that can survive summer drought without the need for irrigation.

To grow your own on a prepared base choose from mosses, ferns such as *Polypodium vulgare* and *Asplenium trichomanes*, and grasses such as festuca, briza, carex, melica and helictotrichon species. For extra colour add (annuals) eschscholzia, gypsophila, linaria and linum; (perennials) saxifrages, sedums, sempervivums and *Euphorbia cyparissias* on thin substrates or alyssum, campanula, dianthus, nepeta, pulsatilla, sisyrinchium and thymus species in deeper conditions. Suitable bulbs include *Crocus tommasinianus*, *Iris pumila* and

I. germanica, *Muscari neglectum*, *Tulipa tarda*, and small-flowered onions such as *Allium flavum*, *A. pulchellum* and *A. schoenoprasum* (chives).

Green walls

Greening the façade of your property might be an easier project than greening a roof. Where a wall is sound, self-supporting climbers like Virginia creeper, ivy and climbing hydrangea can be encouraged to grow freely, their adhesive roots posing a threat only where mortar joints or renders are already deteriorating.

Elsewhere (and for non-clinging species) an arrangement of aluminium or timber trellis battens, stainless steel wires or plastic ropes is attached to the wall, running vertically or as a 50 x 50cm (20 x 20in) latticework, using screwed vine eyes or wooden spacers to leave a 5cm (2in) air gap between the façade and supports for efficient insulation and ventilation.

Plant climbers in large containers, or in the ground at least 40cm (16in) away from the wall: soil conditions there can be exceptionally dry, so prepare planting holes deeply with plenty of added humus. Make sure the finished soil level is at least two brick courses (about 18cm/7in) below any damp-proof course.

Suitable climbers for shaded walls are aristolochia, clematis of all kinds, climbing hydrangea, honeysuckle,

In this small front garden care is largely a matter of pruning and trimming to control the size of plants.

hops and ivy, concentrating on evergreen types in cooler gardens. For warm walls expand the choice to include *Campsis radicans*, climbing roses, grape vines, jasmine, parthenocissus and wisteria, plus Russian vine (*Fallopia baldschuanica*) on the largest walls.

Some of these climbers could eventually cover two storeys or more. Restrain vigorous kinds by pruning them before they scramble beyond reach, or grow more restrained or slower-growing plants like ceanothus, *Cobaea scandens*, cotoneaster, *Euonymus fortunei* cultivars, passionflowers, potato vines (*Solanum crispum* and *S. laxum* 'Album'), pyracantha and schizophragma, together with espaliered or fan-trained *Magnolia grandiflora*, *Picea omorika* and fruits such as apples, apricots, cherries, figs, peaches, plums and quinces.

ROUTINE CARE

Looking after plants in cities is no more demanding than in any other garden, and in an intimate space where you have just a select few to tend it may in fact be easier.

Watering is often the main task, especially if many plants grow in containers. You can reduce the frequency of the need for this by lining porous containers with perforated plastic sheet, and adding water-retaining granules to the

Clematis all year round

Give these choice and versatile climbers shade at their roots and good light higher up their stems, together with plenty of water in a dry summer, and in a sheltered city garden you could enjoy a flower display at all seasons. For winter flowers choose fragrant *Clematis cirrhosa* var. *balearica*. Follow this with *alpina* varieties, then the later spring *montana*s and early-summer varieties like 'Nelly Moser' and 'Niobe'. Late summer *texensis* and *viticella* types extend the performance into autumn, when *orientalis* varieties take over until early winter.

compost; mulch plants with loose materials like bark or shingle, and move smaller pots out of wind and strong sun to control evaporation. Balconies and patios are ideal sites for an automatic watering system based on microporous or drip pipes linked to a main reservoir tank.

In small spaces pruning may be vital to control the vigorous growth of some climbers and woody plants. Every species has a preferred season for this, but as a rough guide prune ornamental plants immediately after flowering and sometimes again lightly while they are dormant, if they need extra shaping or restraint. Trained fruit is best pruned in midsummer to stimulate future crops, and further trimmed in winter to limit size and spread.

Plant disorders

Pests and diseases affecting plants grown in towns are generally the same as those encountered elsewhere, but when plants are few and precious they might seem more sinister.

Warmer sheltered conditions often encourage pests to remain active throughout the winter or appear earlier in spring, although their natural predators will also be on patrol for longer, especially if made welcome in your garden (see panel). Sulphur in polluted urban air used to keep fungal disorders at bay, but cleaner air has resulted in an increase in diseases such as black spot of roses.

It is easy to become unduly alarmed by the prospect of ailments. All plants are susceptible to some disorders, but the incidence will be negligible if growth is strong: robust plants tolerate many problems and shrug off all but the occasional serious attack.

Reduce trouble by sound cultivation: avoid over- and underwatering or feeding, overcrowding, and delay in pruning, dividing or replacing ageing or unthrifty plants. Choose varieties with care, plant them in the right place at the best time of year, and inspect regularly for early signs of disorders. Encourage natural predators and controls by providing habitats such as a small pond, food and water for insectivorous birds and hibernating places for toads and hoverflies.

If problems do strike, first identify the cause: it might be constitutional if the plant is growing in a damp, dark, hot or windy spot. Then decide on your response. Some insects, such as frog-hoppers (cuckoo spit) are a cosmetic nuisance rather than a real threat. But you may have to be ruthless: in a small town garden there is seldom room for frail or unthrifty plants, so isolate the victim for intensive care and then, if it shows no sign of recovery, discard. Some disorders, like viruses, are incurable, while others, such as pelargonium rust, are hard to control on susceptible varieties. Avoid using chemical remedies wherever possible because most also affect benign organisms.

Encouraging allies

Natural insect predators eventually find their prey even in a secluded backyard, but they will arrive sooner if positively encouraged. As well as providing places for them to overwinter, grow plenty of nectar plants for foraging adults. To extend their activities over a longer season, include plenty of early- or late-flowering kinds, like *Anemone blanda*, bergenias, crocus species, hebes, hellebores, ivy, limnanthes, meadow saffron, Michaelmas daisies, sedums, sweet williams, wallflowers and winter aconites.

Expanding diversity is a positive health measure: here herbaceous perennials are reinforced with jardinières and pot-stands of seasonal extras such as ivy-leaved pelargoniums, white marguerites and busy lizzies, silver-leaved senecios and *Lotus berthelotii* with its bizarre 'lobster claw' blooms.

INDEX
Page numbers in *italics* refer to captions to the illustrations